How To Keep

A

Marriage Together

David H. Cruz, M.D.
(Special addition by Sandra P. Cruz, R.Ph)

DEDICATION

I dedicate this book to my parents. Through their dedication and devotion to their marriage and their children, I was able to learn many of life's lessons. Although my parents are recently deceased, their love and knowledge lives in me and will guide me for the rest of my life. I love you both.

This book is also for David, Marissa and Brianna, whom I love with all my heart. I hope that this book will be able to guide them and hopefully will guide their children as well.

Finally, I would like to tell my wife, Sandy, I love you and thank you for always being there for the children and myself.

TABLE OF CONTENTS

INTRODUCTION

HOW TO KEEP A MARRIAGE TOGETHER

I am not one to always come out and express my views, but sometimes there comes an issue that you feel is so urgent and dire that the need to get the message out is so important as to drive you to do the things necessary to convey this point. This is my feeling on this issue of marriage and family. In my profession I see so many broken homes and what it does to the family unit. I see how the man, the woman and the children react and respond to the fall of their empire. Not only does it affect the family itself but it also affects our society. We see each succeeding generation becoming more accepting of divorce and fornication. It appears that the happiness that they hope for is just a fleeting happiness. Marriage has become sanctity for the fulfillment of selfish needs only. But this is hopefully where we turn the tide around. We start with a simple book. A book that I hope will teach a person how to make a relationship work. A hope that our future generations will strive to make their lives and their children's lives better.

This book will tell you about some of the issues that have come up in my life. At times I will discuss some of the issues that have come up with some of my patients that I feel that we can all learn from. As you read this book, try to put yourself in my shoes or in the shoes of those discussed and view your life as well from that point of view. If you are a younger person, then use this book to look into your future. This is one of the tricks that will make you have a better life. I truly believe that if you read this book and try to put some or all of these topics mentioned into practice, you will definitely benefit. Not only will you get a benefit but your whole family will reap the benefits along with you. I strongly encourage you to have both you and your partner read this because, as in marriage, you must go through things together. It will take both of you to understand the concepts presented here to be able to know how to keep your relationship living. I congratulate you in wanting to take steps to improve your life. You should continuously strive to make your life and the ones around you better.

At the end of this book I have included some blank pages, one for each chapter. It will be helpful to take down a few notes as you go and grasp the main idea of every section. It is equally as important to write down what you are going through that relates to that chapter and maybe the aspects of your life that you can strive to improve on. I believe that you will return to this book to look at a line or two and when you do, I hope that you can look at those notes you wrote, maybe five, ten or fifteen years later, and realize that you have done all the things possible to Keep Your Marriage Together.

CHAPTER 1

THE BEGINNING

Let's start at the beginning. I am a Doctor of Medicine in Laredo, Texas. I was born and raised here. I had the fortune of being able to study medicine in San Antonio, Texas which is only about 150 miles away from Laredo. After I was done there with school and Residency, I worked in San Antonio for about 1 year. After that I moved back down to Laredo to start a solo Family Practice.

I come from a family of 3 children. My parents married in 1956 and we were lucky that they remained married until my father's passing. Their bond gave us a good foundation. But a foundation is only the ground floor from which to continue building. Some people use a foundation to build a shelter made of sticks. Others will use it to make a brick house. The choice thus remains each individual's. I would like to think that the sturdy ground floor that was laid out for me has been put to good use.

It seems that the number three has been good to my family. My sister, my brother and I have all had three children. Three I guess is a good number of children;

not too many but just enough to drive you crazy. My sister and my brother took care of driving my parents crazy. I just learned from their miscues and avoided getting into trouble myself. You see, my father was rather military when it came to following his orders. If you were to be in by 10:30 pm and you were not there, then my dad was at the gate waiting for you. I hated those times when my brother or sister did not make it back on time. There were quite a few of those gate parties. But from that I got the benefit from sitting down with my father and talking about what was wrong with not following the rules. I learned how I would have dealt with similar situations and even discussed some of those situations with my dad while waiting for the hurricane to start. I think I played a part in making some of those times a bit more calm than they would have been. This is where I began to learn about keeping calm. I learned that I did not like arguments and that I would try my best to talk sense into people before things would get out of proportion.

I attended kindergarten in a school that was on the same campus ground where my mother's school was. She was a first grade teacher. During lunch I would always sneak out of my class by getting under some of the large tables and then run over to my mother's school to eat my lunch with her. I loved Potted Meat back then and I had that every day. Sooner or later the teacher assistant would come and look for me and take me back. When I was going to first grade, my dad became principal at an elementary school and offered to take me and my brother to that school. He told us that if we were sent to the office, we would be spanked. My brother decided to go to a different school. I went with my dad.

Every morning we went to school it seemed that we would get there late. I guess the teacher's must have hated that. We used to play "Beaver" on the way to school in the mornings. We would find the old VW Bugs and count them. Black ones were 4 points, red were 2 and the rest were 1 point. That was always fun. Once at school I was just another student though. The school was run very well and the discipline was great. Back in the spanking days, discipline was good because of the fear that was instilled into the kids. My father still had many people come up to him and thank him for making them better students and better individuals. There was only one time I almost got sent to the office but I was able to avoid it somehow.

I had three good friends in elementary; one who I hung with from first through third and then two in fifth and sixth grades. Once we were going to be going to Jr. High, we all said we would stick up for each other. My two friends joined football. I had wanted to but I decided not to because I had seen my brother mess up his knees playing Jr. High School football. I saw the pain he went through with the surgery and I did not want to go through the same events. Anyway, one of my friends began to hang out very quickly with guys who would smoke marijuana. That put a halt to our friendship as he got worse as time went on. That was a sad time. I wished that I could have said something to have changed his views, changed his mind and helped him start laying bricks instead of sticks. That did not happen and he did not finish High School. He earned his GED but continued to have drug problems.

In Jr. High I made some other friends that I still keep in contact with frequently. These guys I have come to trust well. There will always be a few good friends that you turn to when times are tough and two of these for me I met here. It is amazing how much we share with each other sometimes and over the years I think it does help. Sometimes though, you have to know when to slow down before you share everything with

3

everyone. At times saying too much can come back and hurt you. We will get into that later but for now let's just focus on friendships. After Jr. High came High School and many new friends. Yet my friends from before were still the main characters in my world. And even though they did change some in order to conform to their surroundings, they always knew where my thoughts were and what my philosophy was in life. That has never wavered. That may be one of the reasons I have turned out the way I am. I always knew more or less what I expected out of myself and what I should not do. I have to look back and know that my way of thinking then really helped me in leading me in the right path.

In Jr. College and then at the University of Texas at San Antonio, my friendships grew. I learned how to deal with roommates. I saw how different each person is raised and what is normal for them. I was able to deal with that well. I can't remember having any arguments with any of my roommates. We always had a good time. After getting my Biology Degree, I did substitute teaching for one semester and then went back to Graduate school in preparation for medical school. Once I was in medical school I knew life would have some dramatic changes in store for me. Not only would it affect my life, but the decisions my girlfriend and I had made at that time all revolved around me getting through school as well. We knew marriage would come only after being able to survive school. One would think that this is where the true story of how to keep a relationship together should start, but I know that this is only the culmination of what had already been. So I will start where I think I should, back in my days as a child.

I remember back in my elementary days that there was a group of children one grade above mine that would use drugs. I remember thinking "why would someone use drugs and be so proud to be using them?" They were troublemakers as one would think. My focus in school, though, became one of trying to achieve good grades. I remember seeing some of the sixth graders get some awards one day. I asked my dad what they were getting those for and he told me it was for their good grades they achieved throughout elementary. At that point I told him that was what I wanted to get when I was in sixth grade. Four years later I was receiving the same awards those kids had received.

School never really seemed hard to me. All the other kids kept saying how smart I was. I would tell them it is not that I am smart but I would spend my time studying when I needed to. I think there was a fear of doing poorly in a class that motivated me. There was also a bit of competition in school to do well. Even when I did not get the best grades, I did not mind. The reason I did not mind is that I knew myself very well. I knew I would succeed in school and in life. As the years went on I kept on seeing some of my friends and others drop out of the challenges of getting good grades. Other priorities would pop up. Priorities like going out, learning to drink beer, being a jock and studying the anatomy of the opposite sex. I was happy with who I was. I knew what I wanted and I knew what I did not want to do. I also did not want my friends to follow in the footsteps of kids that should have done well but made bad decisions early in life, affecting all their existence beyond that point. However everyone has to make a choice. You choose good or bad, right or wrong. I look back now and see how easy it could have been to choose to join the crowd, especially since many of my friends had chosen that route. But by believing in yourself and not wavering from your core values just to fit in, you become a person that can stand alone and make decisions that are vital and know that they will be the correct ones for you. So I saw early in life that choices you make in your young years start building you up, adding bricks to the foundation. This is where you start, at the bottom. You have better start it off well.

When I was in Jr. High, I devised three questions that I could ask myself to make the proper decisions. I began to ask myself these questions because I wanted to make the right decision in everything that I did. I loved my parents and I knew that one day I would be a parent. I knew that I did not want to be a hypocrite and a liar to my future children. So many of my decisions I made were for the benefit of my future children. The first question was very basic; "Is this right or wrong?" Usually one could stop here and continue with life because many things are very clear cut in being either the right thing to do or the wrong thing. But at times the thinking gets cloudy and one would have to go to the next question. Next I would ask: "Would my parents want me to do this?" This question for me was very easy since my parents have good values and I knew what they would like and what they would not. This question however could have some problems for some people. For some children, their parents are their worst role models and if they would ask themselves this question it may end up getting them in trouble. The last question however is the one that kept me from doing a lot of things that I would have otherwise done. I would ask myself: "Would I want my children to do this?" This one question kept me from smoking, drinking and failing. Now one might think that for someone in Jr. High, which is now called middle school, this type of thinking may be too advanced. One may think that these children do not think of the consequences of their actions. But I am here to tell you that if I thought in this manner then it is not out of the realm of thinking that all children could. They just have to be taught to think in these ways.

I believe, looking back, I see the pattern that I developed, mapping out my future. Quietly and without much ado about any one thing, the core of my self was being built. I knew it would pay off eventually. But now you ask what this has to do with marriage? Well, my belief is that when we are young, we are creating ourselves. We are making the mold that we will use in the future. The future of adulthood where we make bigger decisions, decisions that could change our lives dramatically. However, without the initial mold being as good as it can be, the decisions we make may be faulty. The lives we live after our childhood is done can be long and difficult. With patience, life can turn out great. Patience is a great place to start off on the next chapter.

CHAPTER 2

PATIENCE

There is an old man sitting on a bench in the park. He sits from daybreak to night fall. He goes home to sleep and the next day he returns and does the same thing all over again. Every day I go to work I see him there. After 3 years of observing him do this, I decide to go up and talk to him. I want to know why he would spend every day here on this bench. As soon as I ask the question he smirks. He looked at me and said: "I have been waiting for someone to come up and talk to me."

Patience is most definitely a very special quality in people. Some exhibit a very small amount of this necessary trait. Others, like the man above, exhibit maybe just a bit too much. Nevertheless, once you know how patience helps a person in his life, you are sure to be willing to use it to your benefit.

As I have said in the previous Chapter, I have always had confidence in myself. At times I may have had more than at others, but yet always enough to believe in what I was doing. I think part of that confidence also helps a person to be able to wait for something as well. Just as a baseball player has to wait for the right pitch, a person has to do the same in life. You can't always rush into something. Taking your time to evaluate the situation will usually never cause you any regret when it comes to relationships. You have to remember that time exposes the truth about people. Time helps you understand things better. Time will allow you to avoid making mistakes.

My wife and I dated for seven years. Like most people, once you are one or two years into a relationship, you think you know a person well. I am here to tell you otherwise. The truth is that you know some of what that person is like but not all the intricacies. You know the cute stuff and the likable stuff. It is only as time goes on that you will be able to learn about a person well. My wife and I learned plenty about each other even four and five years into our relationship. There is a learning curve in understanding a person. Some may not be learning curves but just a never ending line going up and up. You may want to avoid this type of person. However, once you have had time to really soak in what a person is about, then you are ready to move forward into marriage.

Once you take that step, going into a relationship that will climax in marriage, you should understand that now it is even more important to show patience. Putting yourself in a position to make adult decisions too early in life will most likely end in divorce and a struggle to raise children in the absence of a mother or father figure. I think you know what I mean here. I have seen way too many people engage in sexual relations just because they have a boyfriend or girlfriend and that is what is expected of them. That is what they think having a relationship is all about. This is one of the many flaws that end up costing people too many heartaches. Relationships are to learn about how to deal with the opposite sex. Learn to understand each other. Learn what works and what doesn't. Learn how not to be a jealous person. Learn how not to be possessive. Most of all is learning how to be friends and listen to each other. Once you have a child early in life, there is no turning back. You are now a parent and must act like one. If you have patience, having sex can wait. Once you have the tools to deal with the future, including an education and the necessary funds to have a spouse and children, then that could be the right time to jump into Holy Matrimony and begin a family.

If you do not show patience prior to getting married, you will not have the patience to deal with marriage. You must go into a union with your mind and heart willing to make the commitment, ready to deal with the challenges that are to come your way and take care of them in a way that is beneficial to the family, not necessarily to you. Marriage is not a YOU thing anymore; it is a WE thing. As you begin to have children, then it becomes more of a necessity for you to think of the family first and what the needs are for the whole unit to make it succeed. That is how a marriage must be looked at. It has to be viewed as a single company but with two CEOs. You must patiently deal with everything that comes your way.

There is nothing that I dislike more than seeing young people ruin their lives. It is about at the time that the hormones start going haywire in the body to about the time a teenager grows up to about 23 years of age that they get this weird thought in their head that every decision they make is the right one for them. Even managers of stores have to consult with people to make sure they are making the right decisions. But teenagers somehow know all the answers. It is amazing. So as a parent, knowing this, it is critical to make the time you have with your children, from the toddler years to the time they become old teenagers, as valuable as possible.

It takes rules and reinforcing of the rules to be able to teach your children how kids usually respond at different ages. When you do this slowly and over time, they began to understand what typical behaviors a child or a teenager exhibit are the wrong ones. This allows them to know what is coming their way and exactly what responses you do not want to hear from them at those ages; the most dreaded response being: "IT'S MY LIFE!" Although there is truth to this statement, the fact remains that they probably do not know what the best decisions are for their lives. If they did, we would not have the drug and crime problem we have now. As we know, many love to say that if they do not do something they will never learn from their mistakes. As I have stated before, there are many things we can learn from history and other's mistakes. Some things we will have to learn as we go but no one needs to learn firsthand that smoking can result in cancer or that alcohol will lead to cirrhosis. All we need to do is open our eyes and look around us. Life would be so much better if we would learn from others instead of repeating the same mistakes. We must still be parents and be their teachers, no matter how much they hate it. If you have the patience to teach your child from the onset, it could be that you will not have such a difficult time with them and avoid plenty of conflicts as your family ages together.

I have a patient of mine that showed lack of patience. I guess once the sexual urges start they are hard to stop. Nevertheless, she decided to have sex with her boyfriend. They were a match, she thought, that was perfect. They did not think of breaking up. She had his baby and for a while they raised the baby together. The problem was that they were both still in high school. Soon, the boy saw another girl that he began to like. He left my patient and the child behind to go be with his new interest. That ended the brief relationship of these two. The match that they thought was perfect was now over. Now what is left to be figured out is how the child will deal with the trauma that goes along with the separation of mother and father. The lack of patience that they showed may end up skewing the view of this child as to what the responsibility of a father is and the cycle may continue when the child grows up.

Patience will have to be one of your greatest traits to allow your marriage to grow. You see, not everything in life happens on schedule. My wife and I did lay out our future as we wanted it. However, not everything has happened in the time frame that we would have liked. For instance, in San Antonio we were able to build a house once I started in Residency. My wife was already working as a pharmacist since 1990. When I finished the residency program and when we were ready to move back home we thought of building our dream home right away. Well, right away was not as quick as we would have liked. In fact, it took six years for us to start working on the actual construction of our dream house which we had been thinking about since we had met 17 years prior. Some may have seen this waiting as useless and jumped into another house quicker. This would only have delayed building our house that we wanted even longer or even worse, would have ended our dream of having what we really wanted. With time, things do take shape. Everything falls into line if you follow your goals that you have laid out for yourself and your family. The thing is to have those goals in mind and then accomplish them without straying too much from your plans.

Once you are married, then patience continues to play a big role in your life. You have to evaluate your status and decide whether you are ready for a child. There is no doubt that sometimes pregnancies just happen and if they do, they are a blessing. The good thing is that you then have nine months to prepare. Men have to remember that during this period women go through many changes. Both physically and mentally there will be changes and you will have to adapt to. During our pregnancies, my role was being there for everything that she may have needed. Whether it was going across San Antonio to get a special food that she may have been craving to just being there to listen and give support, I was happy to be part of it all. It takes patience to get through these nine months. Then when the child finally arrives, you will have to learn to deal with the infant and all the nuances that go along with caring for the baby. Sometimes the mothers may get a bit of depression after the pregnancies as well. As long as you are patient, you both will get through this time.

Marriage does offer some other times when patience must be used. Let's face the fact that men are much different from women. Men tend to be messier for the most part. Women are more sentimental. Dealing with the daily routine of the house chores can be frustrating at times, especially if one person does not cooperate with the other. Picking up the dirty clothes, taking off your clothes and letting it fly everywhere for the other person to pick up or doing the laundry can get old quick. Having to do all the cooking all the time, washing the dishes and cleaning the house on your own all the time will become a problem at some point. Over time little things like this can become frustrating. It is important to do several things to avoid these daily chores from becoming a problem in the marriage. First, it is always a good idea to give credit to your spouse to show that you appreciate all the hard work that they do. Next, it is vital that you help each other out at home. It is home for both of you and cooperation in maintaining it is crucial. In other words, no one little item should be allowed to try the patience of the other. When you help each other, there is a great appreciation which is felt, which then helps the marriage.

If there are certain habits that your spouse has that are not detrimental to the relationship but are just annoying, you may want to discuss them together. However, do not expect to have some of these habits to be changed. Some of these you will have to learn how to bear and be tolerant of. Remember that marriage is not a dictatorship. There has to be some give and take and compromising on certain issues. Have the patience to discuss things, understand them and be tolerant of them. If for instance, your husband likes to have his friends over for a football game but you get bothered by it, then possibly you can compromise that they can come over but not to cuss in front of the children or that at those times you will go and do other activities outside of the household. Whatever the issues are, there can be a good solution. You must make it a point of telling them however that certain things bother you but that you are willing to compromise. When you do this it helps so that you both understand each other better and you do not put your patience to the test.

CHAPTER 3

CHOOSING THE RIGHT PARTNER

When do you know you have found the right partner for life? I am not too sure you can always tell at the onset but as time goes by in a relationship you will definitely find out. How did I know my wife was the right one for me? Well, let me try to explain.

My wife, Sandy, and I met in Junior College. We graduated together from High School but did not know each other at that time as she was a graduating junior and we had taken no classes together. In college, we took a physics class together, at least for a while. I had to drop out when I forgot to do one whole page of a test and got a 39 on it. Anyway, during my brief stint in that class, right before that faithful test that got me booted, I went up to my future wife and asked her about how to do one of the difficult problems. I did not know it at the time but she had gotten nervous and directed me to go ask another guy in the class. I did what she said. That however was our introduction to each other, brief as it may seem.

After that time we had a study group which included a bunch of my friends and two or three girls, one, little did I know, being my future wife. Luckily she liked me and another girl that was studying with us liked one of my friends as well. I was rather naïve to the fact that she had any feelings towards me. Sandy one day got the courage to get up from the table from where we were studying and come around to my side. She gently put her hand on my left shoulder. She later told me that she was very nervous when she did that. I reached up and held her hand. After that we began holding hands in class as well. All our friends were trying to figure out where this was going. So was I! We finally became boyfriend and girlfriend and since that time we have been together.

It was six months before I left to San Antonio and she left to Austin that we had made the commitment. Everyone always worries about long distance relationships but I don't think we worried much about it. We trusted each other very much. During the six months that we had together in our home town we learned plenty about each other. I think that we were able to lay down enough foundation to be able to tolerate the time that we were going to have to spend away from each other. We learned each other's hobbies and more importantly learned how to enjoy them together. We began talking about the future, discussing what we would do after school was done. We knew that if we were to get married it would be after we had finished our schooling. We also made our first house plans during those first six months. Believe it or not that also helped us understand each other. It showed us what was important to us, especially with where each of us wanted the emphasis to be in the house. We both wanted a game room and a theater. We both also wanted a small chapel in the house. That first drawing turned out to be a 15,000 square foot house. Maybe just a few too many ideas went into that plan.

During our years away from each other, we visited almost every weekend. It was a great time and I always looked forward to those weekends. Of course we used the phone quite a bit. We used it even more when Sandy found a business that was selling some connectors for the phone line and give us a flat rate for long distance calls. When we were together we did many of the things we enjoyed. We also would take time to talk about the future. I guess at that time they were dreams but I knew they would all come true. All we needed was patience. Luckily she believed me and in the things I would say and we were both willing to wait for the future to unfold.

In some of our talks we would discuss how we would raise our children. One of the rules that we follow even now, which I believe is very important, came from those talks when we were going around. We decided that we would never disagree with each other when one of us corrected a child. **If we did not agree with the punishment then we would discuss it later but not in front of the children.** This has been vital because once children know they can make you take sides then they will use it against you and it will result in arguments in the household. I saw plenty of that growing up. My sister was a pro at that. **We also discussed the fact that we should never go to sleep mad at each other.** We worked on this one a few times during the seven year period that we were getting to know each other. We didn't only say it but no matter how aggravating it may have been to keep this rule, it helped us very much to advance in our relationship. It helped our communication and our understanding of what type of things would bother each of us. It was a learning stage for both of us for which I think we took good advantage of.

Once Sandy was able to move to San Antonio and start to work there, it became only a waiting game at that point. We had to wait for me to get into medical school and become a doctor. Once I entered, life became a bit rougher. During the first two years of medical school there were many students who ended up getting divorced or breaking up with their boyfriends and girlfriends. One student even committed suicide. It was definitely a strain on the relationship with Sandy working and me studying all the time. We went through rough times those first two years but through it all we came to learn more about each other. I believe that it was during our fifth and sixth years together that we knew for sure that we would be together as man and wife. During the last semester of medical school, we got married.

Our year long engagement leading to the marriage turned out to be wonderful. All the details that we had talked about during our years together were beginning to take shape. We both had wanted a big wedding with all our families there. It turned out just the way we planned. I had people telling me years later that it had been the best wedding they had gone to. Maybe it was the open bar that they were referring to but I think that it was the overall planning of the event. That night went by so fast with all the handshakes, pictures and dancing. Our dreams were coming true and being laid out just as we had wanted.

After that night, we left to Vegas for a week. The honeymoon went well. We even made the hotel shake. Well, it was actually a tremor from an earthquake that hit California. It was seven days in a city where people dream. I guess it was the right place for us at the time. It was lucky for us that our dreams were coming true. We were now closer to completing our goals. We both had a college education, Sandy was working and I was only one semester away from becoming a doctor. We knew we had a way to go still but we were having fun accomplishing our goals together. We did it as a team. I did not put myself in front of her and she did not put herself on front of me. We both walked the path together, side by side. In fact, we would each do and still do things that will make the other happy. **We make the happiness of the other person be the priority.** I always think of what will make Sandy happy and then that is what I do. This thinking has helped us grow together and help back each other's dreams so that they become a reality. It is by this philosophy that relationships are able to grow. **You learn that it is not "I" but "WE" that matter. If "I" never comes before "WE", then you know that both of you will help each other make a wonderful family.**

Now that you kind of know how Sandy and I went about knowing we were right for each other, let me mention some other important qualities you must be able to discern in evaluating your partner. Let's also go over some of the things that you should not do or should not be expected to do. You must remember that the partner you are picking is for life and you must choose accordingly. From an individual stand point, you must be confident and not be timid or coerced into a partnership.

One thing that everyone hears constantly is that you cannot change your partner. This is a true statement. I have met some people that have changed their lives completely around after years of self-inflicted hardships. However, this is rare and should not be expected when going into a marriage. You want to know exactly the kind of person you are marrying. The biggest problems come when one partner, usually the male, is a big drinker of alcohol, beats up on his girlfriend when upset or does both of those things. Also a giant problem is when one partner is a drug addict. Remember this, you cannot and should not be expected to change a person. If you marry an alcoholic, then expect to live with an alcoholic. If you marry a drug addict, expect that person to keep using drugs. If you marry a person who has hit you, then expect to be in a relationship with physical abuse. The worst thing you can hear a partner say is "He will change once we are married." Bad habits usually only get worse once you are married. Some people believe that there is no reason to impress you anymore after marriage and dive deeper into their poor choices. A person should be expected to change on their own, way before any commitments are made. You have to be aware that people many times fall back into their bad habits and this could be a problem you will deal with all your life. My advice is never to marry anyone who has hit you. I don't care if you think you love that person dearly. If they have hit you, then they have shown they have no restraint and no respect for you or your opinion. Relationships should never be abusive.

I have seen marriages that have a drug addict and an alcoholic as one of the spouses. They have a very stressful relationship, they lose respect for each other, they fall out of love and they end up separated or divorced. Some marriages do survive having one of the spouses with an addiction, but their lives are usually strained and their children get a very bad example at home, giving them a bad start to life. You see, it is not only about you and your spouse. It is about all your children to come.

Now let's turn our attention to the people that marry persons that have previously been married and have children. This circumstance is unfortunately happening much more often these days. When this happens, the one marrying into the family must know that they will come in second to the children. The children will always and should always come first. Even after you two have children together, the other children have to play an equal part in the parent's life. The parenting does not end just because there is a new spouse.

I hear spouses complain about how the children

from the previous marriage interfere with their plans and how stressful it is to always have to deal with them. I also hear some complain that they are not accepted by the children. The fact is that they should have known exactly what they were getting involved in. Not only is there the children to deal with, but they will have to deal with the previous spouse as well. You all become a big unit to try to raise the children. They marry into an instant family and sometimes it is too overwhelming. Parents grow as babies grow. If you come in to a situation where suddenly you are raising an older child, then you missed out on what it is like to raise a child and are at a disadvantage. Before you jump into a marriage with children already in the equation, make sure that you can handle your spouse having to parent them. Make sure that you will be able to deal with the previous spouse if they are still involved. Make sure that you can deal with the children.

On the other side of the coin, the person with the children should be honest with the incoming spouse. They have to realize what they will be dealing with. Do not try to paint a rosy picture for them and then have it all change. Remember that parenting comes first and if your children do not feel comfortable with the new person, then bringing that person into the relationship may be the wrong move. The opinions of your children must be valued and come first. If you destroy the relationship between your children and yourself, then the joy you think you may be creating with having a new spouse may turn into a life of misery.

When both parties have children, the same rules apply. There is also another twist. The children must also get along with each other. If they don't, then you will have problems. Again, in this situation, uniting the families may be a poor choice. I had an uncle in that predicament. His son did not get along with the new incoming kids. That marriage was quickly annulled. The more people that are involved in the equation, the harder it will be to get it done. Remember not to be selfish in this situation. You can get over not getting married to one person if it is more beneficial to the entire family.

There is one other partner that should never be considered. The partner that I am talking about is the type that is currently married. Never, never, never should one go out with a married person. The reason is obvious. But other than the fact that they are already married, you will be going out with someone that is by definition an unfaithful spouse. That is exactly what you want to try to avoid. If divorce papers are not signed, you have no business to be with that person. The respect that they will have for you will be much less as well. The chances that they will do the same to you are high. I know that the one that is not married thinks that the other person is not the right one for them and that is why this is happening. The unfaithful person will feed them lines to continue the affair. It is usually that they are having marital problems, their spouse does not understand, they got married too young or any other lame excuse. They will do one of two things. They will string the relationship as far as it can go promising divorce is imminent and then never go through with it. They may go through the divorce, end up with you and then you have to live with the fear of being the one that does not "understand" them. This would be a relationship always one step away from disaster.

Another aspect that needs to be looked at is, when someone dates a married person, they can potentially destroy a family. They can devastate the lives of their children and directly impact the choices that they would make as adults by what their parent did. Relationships are not to be taken lightly. The right choices must be made. If the choices are done with the brain and not only with the heart, then you will be able to make better choices.

CHAPTER 4

HONESTY

I can't imagine trying to build a relationship that will work if that partnership is based on lies. Every person wants to know what is going on in their partner's lives. That is part of what brings people closer to each other. It helps in the understanding. It helps so that the relationship will grow. Let's say that a couple is walking together in a large vast land. Now let us add in a twist. Let's say that the woman is wearing a blindfold. With both of you at one end of the land, you must reach the other end together. It is your job to guide her through. In this land, however, there are many areas of quicksand. As her guide through this long walk together, you must make sure that she does not fall into one of these traps. She has to trust you. Now, do you lie about what is the best path to take? If you do, chances are that she will not make it through to the end. This means the partnership and thus the relationship failed.

Lies breed lies. I have seen this plenty of times where people began to lie about one thing. It then becomes easier to do and then it becomes a habit. Once you do this enough then you easily mix the lies with the truth and forget which is which. I firmly believe that this starts in your youth though. Growing up we make decisions that affect us for the rest of our lives. What I have seen is that once a young child lies to their parent once, the next time it becomes easier. As this trend continues, the relationship between a parent and a child becomes more distant. So the object of the parent is to teach the children when they are young to talk to you about what is going on in their lives. But for them to trust the parent, the parent has to teach the child that they do not lie as well.

Parents tend to believe that children don't pick up on these little lies that occur during the course of a routine day at home. For instance, a parent may not think much of asking their child to answer the phone and to tell the caller that they are not home. What has been done is that the child now knows that it is ok to lie about something because mom and dad do it. The same thing occurs if when you go to a store you are given more change than what was due. You could keep it but if you do you will be teaching the child that it is okay to steal. It is no different with stealing cable television or buying stolen merchandise. All these things teach children the wrong things in life. We must be the role models for our children. Everything that we do we must scrutinize to make sure that we are giving the right message. And as we give the right message, we then teach them to be honest. As they grow up to be honest, they are more likely to be honest with their spouse. With this honesty that has been planted into the child, their future relationship may have a better chance of surviving.

I have to tell you about some circumstances where lies have killed relationships and hurt the family. A good friend of mine fell in love with a girl when we were in high school. They made a wonderful couple. They got married very young. Over the years, they seemed to have a good relationship. One year though, and I don't know how, he found out that the child that he thought was his wife's nephew was actually her son. She had apparently had a child before she knew him. That lie ended their marriage. I have had several women come into my office that have been depressed over their marriage. It always seems that they have caught their spouse with another partner. The pain that this selfish behavior causes is many times unbearable and ends up in divorce. Others do not end up in divorce but end up in a very tenuous relationship. They end up not trusting the spouse and in more frequent arguments. No matter how many times they say it has been forgiven, the cheating comes back up in the arguments. Probably this occurs because the reason they are arguing in the first place is because of the lack of trust that was developed from the cheating.

So how are we to become an honest person with our partner? How can we do this if we grew up learning differently from our parents? What if all we have ever done in our lives is to tell lies to get through the day? Well, it starts with a daily process of making sure you stop lying. You need to understand your faults and you need to correct them. If you have been in a relationship and are not married, then before you are married you must be truthful with your partner. You must tell them the truth about yourself. If this ends this relationship then it is probably for the better. This way there is no divorce and no children in the picture. The best thing is that you have learned to tell the truth. Now for the next relationship you will be able to start right from the beginning with the truth. You will find that being honest will help your relationship be more enjoyable. This is true because there is nothing to hide. The honesty keeps people in line. It keeps them from doing things that will adversely affect the relationship. You will think before doing. That is what you want. You want to be able to guide yourself and not have your spouse have to guide you and spy on you. You do exactly what you expect your spouse to do. You expect them to trust you, believe in you, help you and not betray the sanctity of marriage.

Honesty goes a long way in correcting many other faults that you may have. When other parties try to intervene in your marriage, your spouse will know that you are truthful and there will be less doubting involved. I have known couples that have other people who want to see them suffer or get divorced. They will fabricate lies about them or spread nasty rumors intended to hurt their relationship. When things like this happen, you all need to have enough faith in each other to believe that what you all say is the truth. In this way you can protect the marriage from outside interference.

What do you do if you have cheated on your spouse? I know several patients that make this a routine and think little of it. I have personally talked to some of these people and tried to express my point of view and the problems that they are creating for themselves. I have not seen many that care to change their ways. I guess many of these people are not wise enough to know that ruining their marriage may ruin a big part of their lives. They don't see the joy of working together with a spouse and making sure that the marriage becomes a success. They don't understand the damage that they will cause the children. The ones that are already separated whom I have seen in my clinic are always depressed and fighting over the kids. They end up having to defend themselves to their kids because one parent will eventually end up saying something bad about the other. It all becomes a nightmare. So my advice is to not cheat. If you did, then stop! Things can work out well if you are willing to stop and put effort into the family. But it all starts with honesty. If you never say what happened, it may haunt you forever. If you do, then you will have your spouse looking over your shoulder for a while. You should not get mad at that. They are only trying to make sure that the marriage works. The mistake that is done though by the person who cheated is that they get upset at this behavior. You must remember that you have earned that by your bad behavior! If your child one day came home drunk, would you continue to trust them to go out with their friends? Now, the mistake made on the other side of the coin is that the investigations are carried a bit too long and the insecurities remain for a period of time that is overdone. There has to be a point where the trust is regained and that you must believe that your spouse will be honest with you. Do not let it lead to more confrontations. And once you can trust again, do not bring it up again. Begin to move forward in the relationship. I know many couples that have survived infidelity, so there is no need in throwing in the towel right away. If however you are dealing with a habitual offender, you will have a big choice to make.

CHAPTER 5

JEALOUSY

There are many things that can tear up a marriage, but one of the big problems is when jealousy creeps into the picture. Some people are by nature very suspicious. Some have had previous relationships with people they could not trust. Once someone gets to the point of marriage, you would think that trust would not be an issue. You would think that those days of questioning someone's honesty would be far gone. I think that most of the time, marriage does start off with a good amount of trust. How then does jealousy work itself into the relationship? I think it is worthwhile going over this subject.

Personally, I am not a jealous person. I do not see the value of stressing over that. Some feel that if you do not show an act of jealousy when your partner talks to the opposite sex then you do not care about them. Others are overly jealous and the other partner hates it but they cannot seem to be able to change the attitude that is expressed. Still others try hard to make their significant other jealous. Why I will never know. The idea in the union is that you both care for each other. The simple problems that bring about jealousy should be worked out way before marriage should be considered.

By this time it is important that childishness of doubting the infidelity of a partner be gone. If it is not gone by the time you are getting engaged, then do not become engaged! Do not take the next step. Remember that neither marriage nor children trap anyone into a relationship. If you know that a person is not faithful to you or has those tendencies, then do not take the next step. It will only be taking the next step closer to heartache. Remember, we want to reduce the divorce rate.

Speaking from a man's point of view now, we must not give the women in our lives any reason to doubt that we are one hundred percent committed to the relationship. Any flings you may have had in the past are just that, a thing of the past. If however you were not faithful to her when you were her boyfriend, then I doubt that those tendencies will go away if an opportunity comes up where you can cheat on her. I believe that to have someone as a girlfriend means that you would seriously consider that person to be your wife. You choose carefully and if things don't work out or you find yourself cheating on that person, then you should not marry that person. The reason is that you will eventually bring too much strain into that relationship. And if it goes long enough, the strain and problems will trickle down to your kids. So making the right choice is essential. Once it is made, don't ruin it.

How, then, can one learn how not to be jealous and how can you help avoid this feeling? I believe that this answer is twofold. First, you must be truthful to your partner. **Truth breeds trust.** Once there is trust, jealousy can be suppressed, at least partially. When there is a bit of those jealous feelings coming out, then the jealous person has to come out and say what they feel. Do not hold it in. This leads to the second answer to my question. Communication is vital in trying to eliminate jealousy. Constantly talking over situations may help clear confusion in the mind of the partner. It will also help explain what events make a person jealous. The other person can then help by easing the stress of those situations. If they are normal daily unavoidable situations, then you would be able to discuss that those events cannot be avoided but that there is no need for the jealousy.

I have several examples of how jealousy has caused divorce. Most of these can be summed up in two scenarios. One is where the woman is jealous. She is constantly following the person around, asking others to follow him and then confronting him with the situations. In these circumstances, there is usually a good reason to be jealous. It is that they married someone who falls into the category of being a cheater. Most of the time this is known before the marriage but they refuse to accept it and think that marriage is the vessel which will magically transform the person. These marriages many times end in divorce.

The next is the woman, or man, that is extremely jealous of their spouse. Their spouse however does not give them any reason to be jealous. The intensity and the stress of the constant badgering get to a boiling point where the accused spouse cannot take anymore. The continued stress sometimes draws a wedge between the couple and over the years the love that they once shared may be just a whisper of what it once was. These situations may also frequently cause a marriage to end in divorce.

We must work together to avoid jealousy from being a part of our lives. If we communicate, if we learn how to trust, if we know how to respect each other and to do what is right for the partnership, then there should be no need for the "J" word to be part of the marriage. I will tell you something, it is a wonderful thing when you know that you and your partner have the ultimate trust in each other and in the decisions you make for the relationship. It allows the relationship to grow. It helps the partnership expand and over the years you appreciate the value of having been faithful and not having to have put that extra unneeded stress on each other.

CHAPTER 6

SELFISHNESS

I love football! I am a Dallas Cowboy fan. When I was small and up to the time that I was in my early twenties, I would be upset all week if they lost. When I first met my wife, she could care less about football. She however came to learn how much I enjoyed the games. Over the first three years of our relationship, she began to learn all about the game. Soon she was a big Cowboy fan as well. She even learned many of the penalties they would call. By her actions she showed me that she was not going to be selfish. She embraced what I so much loved and made it part of her life as well. She saw that she could enjoy some of the things that I liked. She made the commitment to advance the relationship.

Sandy was the one that also taught me not to be so upset if they lost. It affected the whole mood of the time I would spend with her. Slowly I was able to change my philosophy on how I took those losses. I began to get over the losses in a couple of days. This actually felt better for me to learn how to do this. Soon I would get over it in one day. Now, I just enjoy watching the game, win or lose. I am still just as big a fan. I just have a better way of enjoying the games. I learned to do this for her.

Being in a relationship is hard work. You have to be able to work together and solve problems together. It is give and take. It is having to accept something that you may not totally agree with. It is learning that together you can succeed and do greater things than if you approach those obstacles alone.

One of the thoughts that I have always believed in is that if you love someone, you will do what is best for them. For instance, if someone breaks off a relationship with you and they do not want to be with you anymore, then at that point in time, the best thing is not to be in a relationship with that person. You need to understand that love is a two way street. You can't will someone to be in love with you. This thought works well for people that are not married yet. But if the big step has already been taken, the vows already read, the rings have been exchanged and the 'I do's' have been spoken, then it is your duty to make the marriage work out. Here is where we have fallen so hard. People are just not willing to put in the effort to make a union work. Maybe the beer commercials are to enticing for the guys. Maybe the "clubbing" is too important for the girls. It is one thing, though, that causes all of these problems: **selfishness**. This leads the people to do things for themselves. It makes them do things that make only them happy and not the partner. It separates the "WE" into "I".

One of the most common mistakes that young couples make is that they expect marriage to be exactly the same as when they were single. They do not take into consideration the added responsibility of what marriage actually brings. I see many depressed women because they no longer can go out with their friends. I also see many young men that do not understand why their wives do not want them out drinking with the guys. They do not realize that it is no longer about what makes them happy. Now it is all about the marriage and what is going to make the marriage go forward and succeed. This is what many aspire when they are young. They want to get to the point when they get married. Once they get there, they can only think of how they can please themselves, how they can still prove that they can have fun and do what they want. They put so much effort into this objective that it causes fights in the marriage. Their inability to see their lack of desire to change to help the union becomes a great barrier. The selfishness of their acts becomes the focal point of the conflicts in the marriage. If they do not come to realize that their relationship is in jeopardy over their selfish acts then usually their marriage was in vain. They are only left with the questions of what went wrong.

From day one the objective should be how you are going to reach your goals together. I know my wife and I are very goal directed and want to accomplish everything that we have set out to do. Unlike many couples, our money is put together and used together to take care of all the debts we may have. My debts became hers and hers mine. We became one corporation with one goal in mind: together help create the best partnership possible for the rest of our lives. I know many couples that work differently. The wife pays her way and the man pays his things. Each of them spends their own money. In my case, we deposit everything and from there we find a way to pay everything off.

I was recently talking with my coworkers. They were asking me about what I did for fun with my wife. Other than the obvious, I stated that we liked to do things that involved the children. They were insistent that couples needed time for themselves. I stated that of course we would at times go to dinner together and we enjoyed those outings. I restated though that we did not feel good not involving our kids on our outings. I thought that was selfish. They quickly stated that it was not selfish to take time for yourself and your wife. Of course, I said you need time alone, but when you are trying to show and teach your children that family comes first, you have to lead by example. By choosing to involve them in our activities we are doing this. You cannot teach them that family comes first and then drop them off so that you can go and have fun on your own. The decision was made when you decided to have children. It is part of life.

When you become selfless, you do what is best for your partner. When that is reciprocated, then they will do what is best for you. You will see that as this act is continued through your lifetime, it makes for a wonderful way in dealing with each other. You learn to respect each other and even though you may end up giving up something you may really like, the rewards that are reaped far out gain what you would have gotten if you did things exactly the way you wanted to.

CHAPTER 7

COMMUNICATION

"Shhhhhh! Be quiet! I don't want to hear it." All of these are bad choices of words in a relationship. When someone meets the person that is supposedly the right one for them, there is plenty of sensitivity shown. People are heard out for the most part. Subjects are discussed a bit. As time goes along, the discussions seize. For some reason the importance of hearing one out is diminished with time. If this happens in your relationship while still in its infancy, you would have to seriously question whether this was the right person for you. For it is the quality of being able to hear a problem and trying to work through these problems that helps build a strong relationship.

When a person feels that they can honestly discuss how they feel on a subject, then you know that there is a confidence shared between you both. This, as every other part of a relationship, is a two way street. Communication is made up of one part listening and one part expressing your views. An active interaction of ideas, in a non-combative manner, is able to bring solutions to the questions presented. It is a way of working together. We have to remember that a relationship is both of you together making one decision that is best for the unit. Once you understand that being able to express yourself to one another is vital, you then have to understand another part of communicating.

Knowing when your position is the wrong one and learning how to accept it is very important. Then after realizing that you are wrong, you must express that view to your partner. The reason is simple. They have to know that you understand that you are not correct 100% of the time. If you come to be able to admit to your mistakes and not feel hurt about it, then you have accomplished plenty. I can give you a prime example of this. My friend was going to be starting up a restaurant/bar business. It looked like a good investment. My wife and I were invited into the venture. We said yes. The dilemma was as follows. We began to understand more of the intricacies of the business with the meetings we were having. My wife and I, both being in the medical field and being nondrinkers of alcohol, were about to embark in a venture that did not go along with our core values. How was I to tell a person not to drink and then invite them to my bar? I was ready to just consider it an investment and not think about the alcohol part of it all. Well, Sandy did come back to the values that we cherish. She showed concern and stated that if someone would leave the establishment drunk and kill someone or themselves, it would hang over her head forever. Initially I tried to say that we would not be promoting the drinking, that it was just an investment. But after a short discussion I came to realize that no amount of money gained in the business would ever be worth the agony that we would put ourselves through. I would not be able to honestly tell people to stop smoking and drinking and then provide them with a venue just for that same purpose. It would undermine my treatment of the patients. Not only that, it would also be counterproductive to the relationship that my wife and I have worked so hard to achieve. In this instance I had to admit that I was wrong. I told her exactly that and that made the whole situation easier for me and for her to handle. We solved the problem together.

Another aspect of communicating is that sometimes we communicate what we should not. I know several people that tell me how the spouses' playful criticism of them is very upsetting and bothersome to them. Yet they cannot convey that message to their spouses. Of course the person giving the criticism may not know that it hurts the other person. The offended spouse also has to learn to tell the spouse to stop saying things that offend them. A simple rule to follow is to never criticize a person. Remember that this is the person you have picked to be with you through better or worse. This is the person that will be there for you when you are sick. If there is some aspect of a person that you do not like then try to work on it together in a constructive way. Criticizing someone will not make anyone happy. And once insults start, more are sure to follow. Not only in one direction either. We are all human, and by definition, we are not perfect. So I say to you all, look at yourself first and work on your faults. Work to improve yourself every day. Let others do the same. If you work to become better, others around you will hopefully follow your lead. This will be discussed further in the next chapter.

As we learn to discuss matters within our family, it will help make future points of contention within the family easier to handle. A major rule that needs to be followed during arguments is not to bring up past arguments that have already been settled. If you do learn to deal with issues as they come up as I have mentioned above, then this should never be an issue. However, there are many people that love to bring up the past, not so much to help solve an issue, but simply to help them have an upper hand in the argument. This method of getting the upper hand usually escalates the arguments and is far from being constructive. A person's unhealthy ambition of winning arguments denies them the ability of achieving what in actuality is trying to be accomplished; the solution to the situation. So do not be hung up with winning the argument. If you are not, then you will be less likely to bring up past events that bear no significance to the current topic being discussed.

Some people have an inflection in their voice that always seems to make them seem angry or upset. Some others always talk in a loud voice. Others still are always demanding. There are also those that will argue about every little aspect and complain about everything. These people have to learn and need to want to change their ways. Some don't even know that they are doing it and it comes naturally to them. It would be good to point it out to them that they do these things. Only then will they possibly began to change. It takes plenty of practice to change how one deals with daily life and problems. Being on the other side of this, you must learn to be patient until the change takes place. It may never take place though and the communication may never improve past this barrier.

I would have to advise all of you to practice communication. Work hard to learn how to discuss issues without causing a commotion. Even though I used the word argument above, it truly should never be an argument. It should always be a discussion with a specific goal in mind; come up with a solution to fix the situation. There should never be yelling to express a point as it could hinder the whole process. Many times it won't be easy. Sometimes you will have to refrain from saying things you wish you could. Learn to be constructive and not destructive during these times. Every time you finish with a subject, review it in your head and figure out what you could have done better. If you practice and learn how to do this then it will pay off dearly and save much grief in the marriage.

CHAPTER 8

IMPROVING YOURSELF

How wonderful it must be to be perfect. Sometimes you get the feeling that some people really believe that they are just that. Everything they do can only be done in one way. Worst of all, everything that the person sees you do can only be done their way because their way is correct. We all know that there are many ways to skin a cat, so I think we should discuss this a bit. How does one go from knowing that what they do is correct to admitting that there may be flaws in their thinking? If you look closely at your actions and compare them to what we may think is ideal, maybe you will come to realize that your attitude in certain situations must be changed. Possibly it is a reaction that you have that may need some work and modification. Whatever the case may be, we can all use a bit of improvement in every aspect of our lives.

I examine my actions, my words, my reactions and even my thoughts on a daily basis. I must say that most of what I do I have no problems with. There are times though, that deep thought has to be put into what is going to be said. If you realize that you have said something that is inappropriate, then you must internally deal with that situation. You must know what you said, how you said it and how you would change what you verbalized. For instance, you should never ask someone when their baby is due. You will inevitably run into someone that will tell you that they are not pregnant. One of my friends learned this the hard way. Now she stopped that practice. Other times you will have to deal with arguments that take place. If you do not believe that you handled the situation correctly, then you must figure out a better way of doing it the next time.

Dealing with small situations within the household on a daily basis sometimes offer the most chance for you to make drastic changes in your dealings with problems. When someone spills a drink on a rug, you have a choice on how you will deal with it. You can either yell and get very angry or you can decide to not say a word and just get it cleaned. You can also deal with it in a way that will not make anyone get paranoid. Dealing with problems that are simple in nature should help you in setting the tone as to how you will deal with bigger problems. If you blow your top for the simple stuff, then I would hate to see what would happen when you deal with the real problems that may come your way.

I remember back to when I was a medical student working on the psychiatric ward of the VA hospital. I was leading a support group once and we were having a discussion on what kind of things would make each of them mad. I recall one gentleman speaking up and stating that his wife would make him very mad. I asked for him to give me an example of what kinds of things she would do that would cause him to get upset. He began to tell me about her and that he knew several things that she did were on purpose to get him upset. At the top of the list was that every time she would take the laundry out of the washer and put it into the dryer, she would not pull the pant legs all the way out. He said that she knew that would cause more wrinkles and that would get him fumed that she could not do it his way. This was a prime example of letting the little things get in the way of the bigger picture. In order to have a good marriage you have to realize that small things of this nature should not be blown out of proportion and should be taken in stride. We all have different ways of dealing with laundry, as we do with every aspect of our lives. We must adjust to situations to make life better. Learning this quickly will help you and your family.

As we adjust to each other and learn from each other, we must also continue to grow and become more mature in our thinking. Life is not static, it is constantly changing. We must accept change and go on living. When it comes down to improving yourself with changing times, it is important to realize what your habits impose on other people. What kind of impact do your deeds have on your family? As you understand what they do to it, then it gives you a great opportunity for growth. Let's talk about an issue that affects many households.

Alcohol is a widely consumed beverage by adults and, unfortunately, children. If you take a look at a benefit to risk chart, I believe that what you will see is that there is very little benefit to drinking alcohol but the risk can turn out to be astronomical. First of all, the relationship between the couple suffers as the alcohol many times becomes the one that spends most of the time with one of the partners. The problems it creates with the constant arguments and possibly verbal and physical abuse are not worth the agony of using the drug. The children then see the way the alcohol affects a household and they may end up falling into the same trap. Many alcoholics end up getting divorced because of their inability to do away with the alcohol. Drinking alcohol will never make you a better person or make your family stronger.

I recently admitted a patient to the hospital while I was covering for some other doctors. He had come in to the hospital and had no doctor. Some of the doctors I share call with are assigned to take these patients with no doctor. What I have come to find is that the patients we end up admitting during these times are usually either truck drivers from out of town or drug addicts and alcoholics. This patient was an alcoholic. He would drink about 12 to 24 beers a day. This day he complained of 3 days with abdominal pain. He turned out to have pancreatitis. This was actually his third episode in 2 years. In this disorder the patient gets swelling of the pancreas. When severe, people can die from this disease. With every new episode, it has the potential of getting worse. The treatment is basically keeping the person from eating to be able to rest the pancreas. Because of his drinking, he had caused this problem again for himself. Bluntly I stated that if this behavior continued it would end up being the cause of his death. He stated that he had drunk more because of his upcoming divorce. Is there any wonder why he was getting divorced? Instead of seeing the problem for what it was and try to improve on it, he decided to hit the alcohol even harder. The decision to be made to better his life is clear; stop drinking. I am not too sure that he will heed the advice.

Lucky me, for on the same night I had to admit a man with cocaine intoxication. Once he was alert enough, we discussed his actions and how he was going to have to change his ways. He was already starting to notice some of the changes that happen with cocaine addicts. Paranoid feelings were beginning to be more prominent in his life. In clinic, I have several addicts that already show these long term side effects. Others already are schizophrenic from the use of cocaine. He stated that he wanted to change but did not seem

45

interested in getting help. You have to be able to admit that you can't correct certain problems and once you allow yourself to be helped, it may make all the difference in the world. As you give in to the fact that you are wrong and that you have been doing the wrong deeds, you give yourself the opportunity to change. You will allow yourself to grow and to learn.

If improving for yourself is not something you wish to do, then try improving for the betterment of the family. As you put yourself as a role model for your family, try to always do the things that will reflect well on your family. When you are able to put the family's interest in front of yours, you will see that some of your actions will change for the better. You no longer see the universe from your point of view but rather from your families. As you try to constantly improve yourself, you create a positive attitude. You must remember that having a positive attitude will allow you to view life in a better light with more optimism.

My advice for self improvement is easy. First, you must realize that you are not perfect. You can't always be one hundred percent correct. You do have faults and it is possible to learn from others. If you can admit this to yourself then you are half the way there. Next you have to constantly look for ways to improve yourself. We can all improve physically, mentally and spiritually. Look for those opportunities and take advantage of them. The more you learn how to evaluate yourself, the easier it will get for you to handle similar or trickier situations. You will need to become very good at dealing with problems as you began to have and raise your children. The next chapter will deal with this point exactly.

CHAPTER 9

RAISING THE CHILDREN

This chapter puts together many of the other chapters that have preceded it. Bearing children is one thing. Raising your children is totally different. When done right, you have a chance to succeed in producing good adults that will in turn raise your grandchildren in a wonderful family of their own. Although it is not guaranteed that your teachings will translate into proper behavior by your children, you still have to give it your all. In order to go through the whole process of raising your children, we must start when our children are just a thought in our minds. This is way before the father's sperm fertilizes the almighty egg from the mother.

When my wife and I decided to have children, we wanted to be able to give them the best of what we could offer. We wanted them to have a house, a yard to play in and to be able to buy them toys that they would like. We also wanted to be able to convey our values to them. We knew that the way to do this is to take every opportunity possible to teach them right from wrong. When I say every opportunity I mean every single opportunity that comes your way. Anytime they would do something that was not right, we would want to tell them it was not right. And we knew we could not stop there. In order for children to learn, you have to tell them it is wrong and go further and explain why it is wrong. As we all know, "why" is the favorite question of any child. So as we went through the thought process, we started to learn and teach ourselves how we would present ourselves to our children.

I wanted to be able to tell them stories every night. I thought that this would help them be more creative as they grew. It would also give us time together that they could enjoy and look forward to. It has worked wonderful as my kids still enjoy their stories every night. Together, my wife and I decided a few other rules that we would follow in order to keep parenting as easy as possible without conflicts. The first rule and possibly the most important is to not interfere with each other when one of us is correcting the children. By this I mean that once the decision by one parent has been made to correct the misbehavior of a child, we would allow that to proceed without interruption. Now, once that was done, in private we could discuss whether we agreed with each other or if we should be more lenient on the child. Of course we decided that correcting the children should be done only in an appropriate manner. Discussing the behavior and telling them why something was wrong and how they can do it correctly would be our first option. We do believe in time out but I was also brought up with spanking and I know that is effective as well. Spanking however would be only last resort.

We also wanted to make sure we spent as much

time with them as possible. We know that they grow up very quickly and we would want to have them know that we were there for them for anything that they needed. Just as marriage takes a person in a different direction and changes your life, having children does the same. Children, however, can possibly cause a marriage to go in a different direction as well, spiraling down. This is why it is so crucial to be able to discuss things with your spouse. She or he needs to know that the time that is spent with the child is because you want to be the best parent possible. And while being a parent, you cannot forget to be a spouse as well. Yes it is true that children will come first. We need to care for them and make sure they are raised well. But just as we nurture our children, we must do the same for our marriage. This is why it is so vital to know how you will raise your children. You will avoid hurting each other's feelings. Your spouse will know why you are spending the time doing activities with your child and not spending all your time with them.

We also knew that we would want our children to be able to attend college and we knew that once they were born we would have to start saving money for them. So even during the planning stages we knew that children would be expensive, costing both time and money. But I will tell you this, spending the time planning how to be a good parent gives a marriage a good basic foundation for which to have your family grow and become fruitful. Once your children are born, there is no better feeling in the world. So let's delve into the life of being a parent and together explore all that is coming your way.

Just as in a marriage, commitment is a key to raising children. You have to be committed to put the children in front as a priority. The things that you enjoy have to be, at times, put on hold. Now is definitely not the time for selfishness. You must give your love to your children without any regrets. So you don't go out as much. So you don't go dancing anymore. That is okay. People get depressed or upset about this change in their life and then take it out on their children and their spouse. This frustration is learned by the children and then you and the whole family suffers because of your feelings. We must learn to accept the changes and do the best we can to succeed at them. Commitment is what it takes. You must parent 100% of the time. When one fails to accept that with age comes changing responsibilities and changing lifestyles, you tend to get depressed about any change you are not comfortable with. I tell you now, so listen. Change is inevitable. Change will occur. Take it in stride and accept it and you will be all the better and happier for it.

Sandy and I made a very good decision. All along we wanted to move back home to our home city. We wanted to do this for several reasons. When it comes to children, we wanted them to be raised around a loving family with a good support system. Our parents, their grandparents, would be able to provide such an environment. I saw how my nephews were able to grow up so close to my parents and I knew that with people around you that love you and want you to make the right decisions, it is much harder to go wrong. It makes parenting easier as well when you have the grandparents and family around to help. Not only was it important to have that support, but it was also important for us to have our children grow up knowing their cousins well and to be able to play with them. It is a wonderful goal to strive for to have your children know all their extended family well. As they get older, they will realize how beneficial it was to be in an atmosphere where you are surrounded by love.

As I grew up, my cousins were a big part of my life. Now that we are older, we know each other very well and count on each other's help when needed. It is this kind of relationship I would like my children to get to know and understand. Extended family is an important part of your future, and the future starts with the relationships that are built over the years of your youth. I know plenty of people that could not wait to move away from their home town and live somewhere they could enjoy "freedom". I also know the regret many of them end up with when their family members began to pass away and they never had the quality time that they would have liked to have spent with them. I have also seen how many family members lose contact and all sense of family is lost as the new generation of children is born. I have known children that never really knew their grandparents at all. Depriving them of unity with their extended family teaches them that family is of no importance. And you may expect the same treatment as your kids get old and they move away from you. Maybe then you would have realized what you had done all those years of keeping family away. To teach them the good values of family, one must be part of family. You have to believe in the unity of family being a strong core to the foundation of your children's future.

As the children get older, one would hope that the core values that you have instilled unto them will help them make better decisions. As they began to wander on their own and with their friends, you have to be confident that you have taught them well. If you taught them to avoid problems and to be a leader, then hopefully they will not get in trouble and be able to lead their friends in a good direction. You can't be there all the time to help them, so as a parent you have to have a certain amount of trust. Having trust, however, does not mean you stay out of their lives as they get older. On the contrary, you must get more involved. You must know their friends and you must stay involved in the school that they attend to show that you care as a parent. In addition, you must still lay down the rules at the house. Remember that children do at times become rebellious, where everything they do they believe is correct or even if they don't think it is right they will do it anyway. At these times you must stick to the core values that have been established as a family.

I can recall, as I became older, certain circumstances where my father would allow me to make my own decisions. Even though you can see that he thought I was wrong, he trusted me enough to be able to make a decision that I would be comfortable with. That was very special on his part, since I know how hard it was for him to give up any of that control. Giving children a certain amount of responsibility with choices is smart, but you must be careful. You must not allow them to make ridiculous mistakes. It appears that many parents allow children to make choices that are going to affect them negatively in the years to come. I have seen some parents allow their children to do things that are not age appropriate. Everything that your children do reflects on you and your parenting skills. I know that at times it is impossible to change the decisions that children make, especially when they have powerful influences outside of the home. The effort needs to be made though. We need to be able to express our views and what we believe as well. So how do we go about doing this? Once again, start young!

When children are allowed to do daring things as children, they tend to grow up having a bit less fear of doing certain things. Better put, they grow up not totally thinking things through before doing them. I have seen children been taught in both extremes, some allowed to do everything and some allowed to do nothing dangerous. In both circumstances, there can be problems. What you want to teach your child is a thought process. Say for instance they are going to walk down a hill for the first time. I bring this up because one of the first times I walked down a steep rocky hill I actually ended up rolling down the steep hill. It was not until after I fell that I was told to turn my feet sideways. What you may want to ask your child is what they think can happen to them walking down this hill? If they don't know then you might tell them the consequences of doing it wrong. The advantage we have is that children learn quickly. Then you tell them how to avoid the problems that can occur and the best way to go down without injuring themselves. Then on the way down you show them that there may be divots that may cause them to fall as well so that even if you do it right you may fall. When you do this they start learning this method and after a while they ask themselves the questions. I have noticed this to be true with my children. Now when they play they very quickly point out all the danger areas and know to avoid them. I still ask so that they do not get out of practice.

As they learn how to think things through, they learn how to analyze problems. They potentially learn how to avoid difficult situations and learn ways to deal with life problems that may come their way. It is all about parents teaching. Being patient enough to teach goes a long way. The children will never be regretful of you teaching them how to handle difficult scenarios. The better prepared your children are to deal with life, the easier your marriage becomes as potential problems are averted.

CHAPTER 10

SACRIFICE

You see it every day; someone going out of their way to help another person. Whether it is you running to the car in a rain storm to bring the car closer so that the kids don't get wet or it is you taking the kid out of the theater during a great movie so that the rest of the people can enjoy the feature, it is all about two things in marriage. Sacrifice and compromise. I can tell you that there is no way that marriages can live happily without these two things intertwined in the relationship. But I don't mean that only one person is to be doing all the sacrificing and compromising. This has to be a shared burden. I know plenty of marriages that revolve around the woman doing all of the compromising and sacrificing. These women are not always the happiest. They do not feel as if they have a voice in the marriage. What it takes is both partners listening to each other. Both partners caring enough for each other so as to want to do only what is best for the other partner. When you do what is best for the spouse, you usually end up doing what is good for the relationship.

Personally, I don't mind being the fall guy. I mean, if we are in a public place and someone in my family does something embarrassing, such as expelling gas, I do not mind taking the blame. Why? Simply, it is a way of protecting the family. Protecting their pride and their embarrassment would come first prior to them having to deal with uncomfortable situations. As one cares for his family, you learn that the family comes first. I don't fully understand the people that need to get out with their friends every weekend just to get away from the family. Once you are blessed enough to have a wife and kids, don't abandon that beautiful life. There is no better feeling than being with your wife and seeing your children grow right in front of your eyes, making all the decisions together. No, I can't imagine being away from that.

There are plenty of stories these days where the parents show no sense of sacrifice or compromise. It comes from both the males and the females. I believe that the most obvious of all is the children that have never known their father, or worse yet, don't even know who their father is. These men find it easy to have children and move on to the next woman. Now I am sure that many of these men will blame it on the woman being too possessive, causing them to want to stray away from making any form of family commitment. I can't necessarily buy this argument. The biggest reason I do not buy it is that the man was more than glad to have intercourse with this woman, either knowing she was possessive or not caring if she was or was not. That in itself is already a sign that the male was not in it for the long haul. In fact, indiscriminately sleeping around proves that there is no serious attempt to be a father and if it so happens that they do become a father, they will look for an easy out of the relationship.

Now there is a flip side to this as well. Some women are very possessive. Some women do not want to compromise on certain things. These are signs of mistrust. The whole basis of the relationship is in question when there is no trust. Why on earth would a relationship such as this be started in the first place? I know that it really takes practice for some, and the learning curve could be prolonged, to be able to master the art of trust, happiness, sacrifice and compromise. But the point I want to get to here is this, once a terrible relationship breaks off with no father figure in the picture, and the woman stays with the children, this is a time when a woman needs to show the sacrifice and commitment. It is the commitment to the relationship with the children that is vital. Here is where we see so many young women falter. They believe that since they are still young, they can go and do what others do. They long for the partying, the dancing and just having a good time. However, the children then are the odd ones out. This is the selfishness that is shown by these women. They will have their fun at the expense of their children. The objective is to never have it come to this point.

So it takes both parents to be mature. Both parents must understand marriage and family. It is only together that a family will survive. It is only when a man and a woman work together as one unit, and knowing that divided they will fall, that the relationship will work. And so there are sacrifices to be made. New things are to be learned. Old habits and routines must be abandoned. New ideas have to be appreciated and accepted. Two separate dreams of the future must be combined and coalesce to form into one common goal. How else will you achieve happiness together?

CHAPTER 11

ACHIEVING HAPPINESS

So how does one achieve happiness in a marriage? As you can see by the previous chapters, achieving happiness is hard work. But the fact is that when done right, happiness comes to you. Many times you are the one that can be the igniter of the good feelings that bring about happiness in how you deal with different situations or crises in the family. It is all a matter of being prepared. For example, we have all been taught in driver's education how to respond if our hood pops open when we are driving or how to deal with a blowout of your tire. I try to always think ahead when I am driving. I think of unusual situations that can occur so that if they do happen, I will know what my actions will be. Just as it helps behind the wheel of a car, preparation in dealing with issues in the family helps. If you are able to keep a cool level head when bad times occur, the family will sense that. They will soon learn to deal with those situations as you have done. It allows for the rest of the family to follow your lead. I always try to keep the family smiling. Even when I get upset at one of my children, I get upset only for what they did wrong. I try not to yell or become upset at the other children that did not have the blame. Then, after I am done, I can speak normally to them about another subject and move on. You leave the misunderstanding behind, already having made your point. So the mood is yours to set.

If you were to ask someone, would you prefer happiness or sadness? Which one would they pick? Hands down happiness would win. So why do some people seem to want to de depressed? Why do others just want to argue? Why is it that some can't stand to lose an argument and always want to get the last word in an argument? Aren't these practices detrimental to happiness? I think they are. Granted, it is impossible to be happy all the time. But I think that is one of the reasons we have a marriage, so that when one half of the equation is down and out, the other half can pick it right up. We have to put plenty of faith in a marriage, which is why making sure that you are with the right person is vital to the future happiness and success of the unit.

Just today I was talking to a patient who had walked out on his wife after ten years. While she was out on the day prior to her birthday, he packed up his stuff and moved out and went back to his home city. He stated that the stress was too much. Health wise, he stated he felt better now than how he was doing while in the marriage. The financial burden was too much as he was having to pay the bills of his marriage, the mother in law's bills and at times the bills of the sister in law. When he brought it up with his wife that he did not want to pay these other bills, she got angry. If his portrayal of this situation is accurate, and at times hearing one side of the story is not completely so, then this situation did not lend itself to be a creation of happiness. It sounds more like a marriage of convenience for the wife. All the help was for her family and no appreciation of the destruction it was creating for her marriage was considered. It would seem that her inability to view this as a problem created a bigger problem; the demise of the marriage.

One of the good things about my wife and I is that we like to be there for our families when we are needed. We both believe that helping the family out in any way is an asset for the whole unit. It also sets a good example for what families can do for each other. Hopefully everyone will understand that the success of the family will continue to breed success in future generations. Whenever possible, if needed, we do not mind helping out financially. For instance, offering our house in San Antonio free of charge for Sandy's brother and sister while they attended college was something we were able to do. This saved everyone money. I do have to thank my parents because I think that it is from them that I received the teaching to be giving to the family. They continuously helped not only me but my brother and sister in any way that they could. I know that my life is better because of their help and this is now what we want to do for the rest of the family. We want to be able to make life better for everyone. Happiness within the family and harmony with both Sandy's and my family is good. We don't see it as helping out one over the other. When there is need and we can help, it is our choice to help. We always discuss it first and make sure we agree though. That is vital. Helping family is second nature and if the intention is good then there is no doubt that the deeds will be embraced. I bring up this topic of giving here because I find that when you are able to give, it promotes happiness in the marriage. Greediness, on the other hand, gives growth to anger and arguments. I believe that if you are in a situation to help, in any way and not only financially, it would be a good idea to do so if the result is for the betterment of the family.

Happiness does come as a result of everything working together well. Having trust in each other to make things work is vital. Having respect for each other's opinions and actions is necessary. Helping your spouse out to help the family unit also helps to make things run smoother and is always appreciated. Achieving happiness is a wonderful goal to have. The optimism it provides for the relationship and the family is a positive influence which will reflect well on the family and possibly inspire others to strive for the same goal.

CHAPTER 12

SEXUAL RELATIONSHIP

How can we go on any further without mentioning one of the most important parts of a marriage? We can't. It is time to get on with it and discuss the intimate part of our relationships. This is one of the most important aspects because it is where much tension of the relationship is either caused or released. The sexual relationship between a husband and a wife is vital, but, for some, it is not as essential or as important as it is to others. So how do we know if our intimacy is helping or hurting our relationship? Let's go through this, breaking it all down, in a very nonsexual manner.

First we should mention that of compatibility. For some of us having a lot of sex is once a week. For others, a lot of sex would be two to three times a day. For most, it is probably somewhere in the middle of these two. Whatever your desired sexual frequency is, you must also consider the sexual frequency of your partner. We also need to understand that over time, the amount of sex a person will want to have will vary. There may be times that a person does not want to engage in sexual behavior and there may be times they do not let you rest. So how do we know how often and when? Well that can easily be figured out by communicating with your spouse. Open and honest conversations as to your preference will make it easier over time. It will probably save moments of frustration later. For instance, I know of several marriages that have broken up because of sexual frustration. One person wants to have sex more often and the other does not feel that sex is important. This becomes very frustrating. Even though you wish these marriages do not break up as they go through 'better or worse' together, they often fall apart. I know of a marriage where the wife does not like to have sex and the husband has put up with it. He is a very frustrated man indeed, but he has to be complimented on his endurance and ability to handle the anguish that he feels.

So compatibility with frequency is important. In addition, respecting each other is also very important, even during sex. I say this because certain practices may be viewed by one as something they would want to do while the other would not like to participate in the same activity. Also, if your partner does not want to be active on a certain day, then that has to be respected. You can't get upset over this. You must understand that you cannot get your way in this department all the time. If you do get upset, then this sometimes becomes a cycle. What it then causes is insecurity and ill will towards each other as the other partner feels that they need to have sex with you just so that you don't get upset. Then your spouse is not really enjoying the moment, merely going through the motions. The sexual relationship is supposed to be a wonderful experience enjoyed by both. Be cognizant that understanding each other and respecting one another leads to a more healthy sexual relationship, and in all, a more fulfilling marriage.

There are times in life when stressful situations put a halt to the sexual urges. This is common and must be taken into consideration. Different medical conditions will also hinder sexual relationships. Medications will sometimes decrease the libido of individuals or cause erectile dysfunction. Some of these situations are stressful. When a man is not able to get an erection, it becomes one of the most sexually stressful events he can go through. Understanding is vital, and not jumping to conclusions is even more important.

When there appears to be no logical reason for the lack of an erection, a man begins to worry. If he comes to the point that he is worrying about whether he can get or sustain an erection, he usually will not be able to have one. He then gets even more worried and stressed out. It's a vicious cycle. Now, on the flip side, the woman usually starts to believe that she does not get him excited anymore. That is the worse conclusion that can be arrived upon, but it is probably the most frequent. The woman sees herself as a failure and gets depressed. Even as the man tries to tell her that it is not her, she does not seem to buy it. I have seen this in clinic many times where the man wants me to explain this to his spouse. As a doctor, I go forward and explain the different reasons for erectile dysfunction. We cover the fact that stress and fatigue have much to do with it. I also mention that alcohol can cause problems as well. In addition, I have to worry about peripheral vascular disease and go over questions and conduct tests that help determine if the man needs to be further worked up medically. If it is psychological, reinforcement is usually all it takes. If man can have morning erections, then that is a good time to be able to get the confidence back and the best to have relations. These days, sometimes you can give them back the confidence by giving them one of the few impotence pills available. The main thing here is for the woman not to get depressed over the situation and work for the resolution slowly. Rushing will only make things worse.

So what about as we get older? The hope is that you grow together in the relationship and by the time you are in your older years you have a pattern that you follow. However, problems do arise. For women, as they go through menopause, vaginal dryness becomes a problem. Lubricants must be used or hormone replacement given. Starting the penetration however has to be done slowly until lubrication is to the point where it becomes less of a problem for the woman. If this is not done then it may cause very painful sex for the woman. Special considerations will need to be taken. For the man, as they age, they may still be able to get an erection but the duration or stiffness may not be the same as before. Sexual understanding must be done mostly thorough communication and understanding. Patience also plays a big role. Medical advice and consultation is many times required and I encourage you not to be shy about this topic with your doctor. That is what they are there for, to be able to help or resolve the situation.

One last brief topic merits discussion in this section. How does anger affect sex? Anger will most definitely take away some of the luster of a sexual relationship with your spouse. If anger is what is expressed to your spouse and this anger is not dealt with in ways to resolve it, then the beauty of the intimate relationship will be tarnished. Many times the sex will have no meaning for the spouse with the anger. Or it could lead to no sex at all. This is one of the reasons that anger has to be resolved. You should not go to sleep angry. You should not carry anger with you for long periods. You should prolong arguments by adding new topics that are not vital to what you are currently mad about. As you learn to work out your anger and resolve issues, then the whole marriage, including sex, gets better.

CHAPTER 13

DON'T RUN AWAY FROM YOUR PROBLEMS

Many times we do not want to face up with what is actually going on in our lives. We feel that turning the other cheek will do just fine and will result in you not having to deal with the problem. When met with a problem, the best thing to do is resolve it. If you don't, it will linger and never go away. It is similar to a man coming up to a raging river, having to get to the other side. If he decides to go away and come back tomorrow and see if the river is less dangerous, then he will always be doing that. The river will not be going away. Now, if the man who needs to get to the other side starts building a bridge, he will hopefully accomplish his goal.

Problems are just like this river, they cannot be avoided. You must find a way to build that bridge to get over the problems. Look to see if there is a way to deal with what is causing the problem. Getting to the root of the problem is important to be able to solve the situations that may arise.

There are many ways that people turn away and try not to deal with the reality of a situation. I see this everyday in my clinic. The biggest problem I see is probably alcohol. Too many are turning to alcohol when they are in some sort of stress. The problem is that the stress is still there after you are done drinking and you still have to deal with the problems. I recently admitted a patient with cirrhosis that started drinking again to solve his problems. The only thing it did was cause him to get a bleeding ulcer in his stomach and a blood transfusion. What a problem solver that alcohol is! Others get depressed and turn to alcohol as well. This is where we see many people attempt or commit suicide.

Other times people want to just leave the house and not argue. Some prefer to say 'let's not argue' and refuse to hear the other person out. It's great not to argue, but if there is no resolution, then it worsens the situation. So how are we to make these people that refuse to deal with the reality of a situation come to the table and discuss what is going on? We do it exactly like that.

We must first realize that yelling between adults does not resolve a situation. In fact, I propose that it makes the situation worse. As the other person may become insulted that you are yelling at them, they feel the need to defend themselves. Dealing with a problem has to be done with clarity and focus. You have to know what the problem is. You need to know where everyone stands on the situation. You need to know the pros and cons of the problem that you face. Then, together, you decide on the best outcome. The point of discussing things out and together making a decision is very important. This is not a controlling factor as many would want to believe. One person does not control the other but merely a decision is made together to help the situation and the marriage. Remember that it is not "I" but "WE".

If there is a problem that is secret and held from the other, this may present a problem. If there are instances from the past that in reality bear no significance to the marriage, those are best left behind and forgotten. Too many people get hung up on the past. If it is something that your spouse would get upset about and will find out about, then it is best to come from you. A marriage should never happen unless a person knows everything that can affect that marriage and is forthright about the past. If you know everything about a person's past then there is no need to get upset. If occasionally things do pop up, as no one is perfect, then it is a matter of dealing with it together and getting over it. Forgiveness is vital.

Sandy and I will usually take on our problems that we face. We talk about them and then make the best decision possible. Of course the weight of the discussion always is more on the person that is directly involved in the situation. If it involves both of us equally, then we do what is best for the marriage and family. We have learned that there is no problem that is too big for us to handle together. We love and respect each other. We know that life is a long road to be traveled and that we chose to travel through it together. We look forward to the future and as things pop up, we support each other. Through it all, we have our never ending faith in prayer that helps us cope with the situations presented to us. For those that lack faith, you should try it sometime. It is a wonderful and powerful feeling that keeps you going and helps to guide you to make the right decisions in everything you do.

There are plenty of irresponsible people. Let me mention a few that I have seen. I would mention that I believe that having intercourse out of marriage is irresponsible. For the men, it may lead to having contracted the virus that is more associated with causing cervical cancer. Even if your spouse has never had intercourse, you will give her a disease that may kill her. Then you worry when it is too late. For the women, running the risk of pregnancy or contracting a disease is a big problem. Raising children with no father is a very sad situation, not to mention all the diseases that are being passed on to everyone.

I saw a woman in my clinic that was pregnant. She had just missed her period and was about 8 weeks into the process. She came with all the knowledge the internet has to offer as to how to have an abortion. I was not going to be dispensing any medications to someone who was already pregnant. She was going to have to go to a specialty clinic, none of which were in town. I told her that I believed that the best thing was to carry out the pregnancy. She said that a baby did not factor into her life right now, with school and work being primary at this time. I looked at her and told her then to stop having sexual intercourse until she was ready for that type of commitment. The worst thing is that the boyfriend also wanted to end the pregnancy. If this does not bother them now, it may cause problems for them in the future. But this kind of careless behavior is very common these days. You could only hope that this stops being one way of running away from your problems.

On the other hand, I have a younger patient that follows up in clinic. She became pregnant and initially wanted to get an abortion. She quickly then changed her mind and decided that to do that was not the right thing. Getting pregnant was not the smart thing, but her handling of the situation was very appropriate. She has gone on to finish high school and is now in college. I am very proud of her, the way she has stuck to accomplishing her goals even though she has had to do it the hard way. You could see her grow wiser every year. I would hope that she will be able to pass on her knowledge that she acquired and be able to change the lives of others by convincing them that premarital sex is not the way to go.

In short, confronting the problems that come your way will help you in various ways. I would hope it would help keep your marriage on a good level base. Knowing, that discussions between the partners are vital to accomplishing your goal of problem solving and staying married, sets a good foundation for you to grow from. This is important not only for you, but for the whole family.

CHAPTER 14

MONEY

Along with lack of honesty and infidelity, money has to be one of the major issues in a marriage. One doesn't always think of this at first when you get married. Many are idealistic and believe that love will carry them through thick and thin. It may very well do that, but at some point, if there is no money to back up that love, there may be major arguments. When the bills are not being paid, the water and light are being cut off or when you can't afford to buy food, the reality of money comes to light. Other times it may be the luxuries of life that you will miss, like cable television, going out to movies or even going out to eat at restaurants. In every marriage, at some point, finances become a topic.

Sandy and I made sure to finish college before we got married and had children because we knew that we did not want money to be a big issue. Nevertheless, it is very easy to get carried away and spend your money on foolish things. We have been guilty of this. Every time we think we have learned our lesson and decide that we are going to be cutting back on our spending, we look back several years and think; "What were we thinking spending our money on that?" But even through that, we move forward and try to learn from our mistakes.

What are the main things that you have to spend your money on? Well, first of all you have to make sure that you have enough for your basic needs. The bills, the mortgage, clothes, food and transportation are definitely basic needs. Once this is taken care of then you have to take care of having health insurance for your whole family. I have seen too many people wiped out and put into severe debt from only one hospital admission. Buying insurance may seem like a waste at times but it is a definite necessity to have! Once you cover the health insurance issue, then you have to look at the other types of insurances.

What would happen to your family if one day you were injured and were not able to work? I know plenty of people in this situation that I follow in my clinic. Depression is where most of these people end up in. That, along with overwhelming anxiety as to how they will afford to live and pay their bills to support their dwelling place is what ends up destroying them. It is for this reason that you have to consider very seriously obtaining disability insurance. If you were to become disabled, then this insurance would kick in and be able to keep you and your family on your feet. This topic needs to be researched further by you so that you can make an informed decision on obtaining this type of insurance.

Next, we have to deal with life insurance. When is this a good thing to have? It is only necessary to have for a couple of reasons. The first and most important is if you have a family which you need to support. If you die, you would want enough insurance money that your family could set aside to be able to continue to make the amount of money, off of interest from that amount, necessary to maintain their needs. You also would want a certain amount of money that could be set aside that can make enough money to get your kids through school. As the years go by, the amount of life insurance that you need will change, usually decreasing as you get older and have less debts to pay off. This needs to be addressed frequently by you and by your life insurance broker. Since there are many types of insurances that are offered, it will take some studying on your part to make sure to obtain the type that is right for you and your family.

From your salary, it will also be imperative to save for the future. Many companies have retirement funds. If where you work this is not one of the benefits, then it will be in your best interest to be able to save into an IRA, ROTH IRA, stocks, bonds or any other avenue that will be able to provide a future income for you. It is always important to be able to save money for your future first before spending your money on anything else.

As you can see, even without any luxuries, life is expensive. It will take plenty of money to be able to take care of your family for the future. So don't make rushed decisions to get married too soon or to start a family too quickly. Then, when you do have the money, learn how to spend it and think about how your money is being spent. The one of you who is the best accountant should keep track of the finances. Both of you should however be aware of how the family estate is coming along.

I know various couples that each keep their own salary and spend it on themselves. I think this is counterproductive to a family creating unity. Sandy and I consider the money I make and the income she makes as one income for the family. All of it goes for the betterment of our family. My bills are her bills and vise versa. That is why it is important that spending of money is done appropriately and well managed. Once we are able to clear the bills then we have money to do stuff for entertainment, within limits. Working together to make the family financially wealthy is the best way to accomplish financial stability for the family and avoid money arguments that may be detrimental to the marriage.

As you begin to amass wealth, it can become addicting. Along with all the things that you must accomplish with your money, it is vital to remember one thing. Family always comes before money. It is imperative to make time for the family in every way possible. I have seen many, men especially, working constantly and putting in overtime to be able to bring home money for the family. However, the relationship with their spouse and with their kids begins to suffer. After time, the person continues to work overtime, but now it's to pay for child support. Unless you have a spouse that understands why you are putting in the hours and can be constantly with your children, then I would have to recommend against any person trying work to this end. You have to have an agreement with your spouse as to what the plan is and if there is not one then you must cut back together and live with the lower income. It is better to live with a lower income than to cause your family to fall apart.

Mistakes can easily be made when you begin to see money. Sometimes everything looks like a great investment. If you begin to put money into everything, you will inevitably look back and see a trail of mistakes. Poor investments, useless purchases and unaccounted for spending will occur. In order to avoid this, which I will tell you now is very hard to do, you must be organized and keep good track of your money. One of my friends is a master at this. The years he does keep track of it, he will break down his spending into percentages. He will know how much of his money is going to leisure, groceries, house expenses and other allocations. When you do this you are able to realize just how much you can actually try to invest without it becoming a big issue for the family. The more you are organized, the more secure you will feel about the money and the more careful you will be as well as to where you spend it. Once you become organized and know how much of your money is going where, you can feel more at ease. You learn not to overindulge in one aspect of your life if it puts you in a squeeze in any other part. Or you can decide to take some money from one area to use it for another if it does not interfere with the bigger picture of placing your family first.

Vacations take money as well. Whenever possible, trips should be planned well in advance to be able to pay the debt off easier over time. For instance, when we planned for our vacation to Disney World, we made sure that we had it all planned out a year in advance. This helped us in that we were able to pay off the trip well in advance of taking it. By the time the trip came around, we did not worry about it. Most of the trip had been paid. Once we came back we had no expenses that we had to worry about. Sometimes, though, one has to make unexpected trips or expenses. How do we handle these? If you are lucky and planned for such unexpected occurrences, then you have nothing to worry about. But what if you did not plan for anything of the sort? What do you do? This is the time where you want to have a good relationship with a bank officer and a history of good credit to go along with that.

By working closely with a bank officer, you are able to develop a relationship that may benefit your family greatly. By slowly working to get good credit, you can help your bank be able to trust you and help them to lend you money with no fear. It is in times when the unexpected comes up that you might be able to be bailed out by your banker. Of course if you have a good relationship with your extended family and they can loan you an amount that you will pay back, then that may be the best scenario. But even if that is the case, you should work hard to have a bank be able to back you up.

CHAPTER 15

LIFE CHANGES – CHANGE WITH IT

When a relationship starts, most of the time it is a wonderful experience. There is a feeling of warmth and caring that makes you feel special. That feeling is what we always want to feel throughout a marriage. How is it that over time it is lost in some relationships? I know that it can be maintained, but you have to understand how life changes over time.

There is a continuum in life that everyone must go through. In the end is death. In the process of going towards our final destination, you could make marriage a wonderful experience on that trip. Knowing that you will change over time, you must understand that a relationship also changes over time. As you go through life's changes, the marriage that you started with can be as strong at the end as it was in the beginning. When you grow old together, you learn from each other. You learn what each of you need and mean. I know that sometimes it just takes a look and the spouse already knows what the other is thinking. There comes to be a deep understanding of each other. This is one of the beautiful things about being together. Through each step and each change, you must understand why the changes have happened and how to adjust to the changes.

I know some couples that have stayed together, married, but hate each other. I almost can't imagine why they would put up with each other, but I believe that under the hate and the arguing that occurs, they still see the original person they married. They see the one they will feel sorry for when they pass away. The part of that person that they will miss when they are gone is the one that they stay for. It is so easy for people to argue at home with the ones that they love and the ones that they are comfortable with that they forget that they are hurting them. As you go through life, you have to understand that it is necessary to keep arguments away from interrupting a marriage.

Other problems build up over time as life changes and may also cause stress in the marriage. Issues should always be resolved as they come up so that the relationship can continue to move forward. The problems at times may seem trivial to one partner but to the other, they may be a large obstacle. Everyday can bring forth a new circumstance. Every year that passes can also bring to the forefront feelings and thoughts of what you expected out of life and the actual life you are living. We all have dreams. We all want to live the ideal lifestyle. We should all strive to be better every day and as we go through the years, we should be happy that we have done this, even if not every goal is met. It is important to be accepting of life as it comes your way. Accept change as we get older. Talking about being older, one of the aspects of life that many have trouble with is getting up in the age.

It is probably in the thirties when a person starts to realize that they have to begin to get checked by a physician. That is when the worries of family history begin and when people want to try to get back to how they looked when they were nineteen. There is some anxiety that goes into this time as you may be started on medications or be diagnosed for the first time with a chronic illness. For some, denial sets in. It never ceases to amaze me how scared people are of taking medications "for life". That seems to be the biggest fear. I try to explain to them that it will hopefully prolong their life and then hope that they comply with the medications. The fear that lawyers have put into people is also amazing. The cholesterol fighting drugs are always feared by people because they can harm the liver. Of course, when taken appropriately and abiding by routine checkups, all the problems can be avoided. Those fears are really over done as most people do great on these medications. However, I always have people that are afraid. I sometimes then ask them if they drink alcohol. When they reply 'yes', I ask them why they haven't worried about the alcohol killing off their liver. Alcohol has a greater chance of ruining their lives, both emotionally and physically, than any medication made to increase your life expectancy. The problem is how both drugs are perceived. Anyway, I'll stop my rant now and simply say that changes occur. We have to be able to put up with them and deal with them and then not over dramatize the event and make the whole matrimonial relationship be about your medication or chronic illness. We have to adjust to the changes in our bodies and not let it scare us. Both you and your partner will be experiencing changes and together, but, with each other's support, you can make these changes much smoother.

Every decade brings about changes. Midlife crises may happen and menopausal changes will eventually occur. The changes that happen before then are sometimes more subtle but may be more devastating. Attitude changes, philosophy changes, becoming more knowledgeable, all which can have a profound effect on your marriage. New working environments, unemployment, new friends along with other stresses in life can impact your union as well. Everything that comes your way, you will have to learn how to deal with it together. The key is not to deal with it by arguing, but by going over the issues, knowing what is the best way to approach the issue, support each other and then work through the changes together. When you are able to do this well, without any arguments, then you have learned how together, as a couple, you can deal with the changes in your life. This definitely takes both of you working together for a common goal of keeping the marriage strong.

CHAPTER 16

DIFFERENT RELIGIONS

Religious differences in relationships are difficult to tackle. There are very few options when dealing with this subject. One person will either convert to the other religion or one is religious and the other is not. The one with the strongest beliefs will most likely be the one to decide what religion the children will be. However, what if both people have strong convictions for their religion? What happens then? Let me go through a story that may help everyone out there.

My best friend, a Christian, fell in love with a wonderful young woman. She was Jehovah. Just when it looked as if the relationship was not going to happen because of her family's beliefs, she decided to leave and start a life with him. Thus, a wonderful relationship began. Before they were married, my friend and I discussed how difficult it would be for two people with different beliefs to be able to be married and make it last. We also talked about the concerns of the children that may come in the future. My thought was that if she was the one that would be going to mass and continue her religious beliefs, then their children would probably be of her religion. That in itself was not bad, what I had concerns about was whether he would be okay with the fact that in an emergency, his children would not be able to get blood products given to them. Nevertheless, they got married and lived together very happily.

Over time, in everyone's life there is change. In the marriage of my friend, change occurred. When one is young and does something out of love, the thoughts are sometimes not completely processed. There is a time rebellion gets the best of you. In leaving your home, you move on and do what you think is best for you. Sometimes as a teenager, no matter how mature you believe yourself to be, you can still be wrong in your judgments and decisions. She not only left her home, in a way she was separating herself from her religion. With this taking part, the whole perspective of her existence was to change. She did need to keep some connection to her religion, but it was not going to be through her parents. She needed to continue her beliefs on her own. My friend had to respect that she would continue of the same religion, and he would his. That would only be fair. Through that obstacle, they would have to keep the common ground that held them together as a couple. Hopefully that would be enough for the marriage to succeed.

As with any rebellious stage anyone would go through, you eventually begin to come back to your roots. As you become more mature and begin to make the decisions that seem right in your heart, your mind and in your beliefs, you come back to where you once began. And once you arrive in that very familiar place, you begin to make those decisions that coincide with your beliefs with more conviction. You gain strength from having traveled the road that strayed you from your path. You have learned that maybe your decisions were not the best and you realize that your direction in life is going away from where you thought it would lead you. So too did it happen in this relationship. Once the religion, the following, came back strong for her, there was nothing that could be done to change the outcome, short of him converting. Changing cities closer to home did not help the situation either. Being closer to her family helped her to be closer to her beliefs. A little over ten years after it started, it was over.

You never wish a divorce on anyone, and having my friends, who I never thought would be getting separated, go through this ordeal is traumatic. I can tell you this, these two are wonderful people who I love very much. Religious beliefs aside, they would have lasted. Maybe they can find themselves in the future and come to some understanding and work things out. That we will leave for time to tell us all.

These two wonderful people are why I have added this chapter to this book. Through their relationship, much can be learned. As I told my friend, there is nothing to feel sorry about. They both lived wonderful lives together and helped each other though rough times. This experience has been good for both of them. We also, as they did, can learn that religious beliefs are very powerful. I would have to say that if you met someone of a different religion and planned to take the giant leap into marriage, you must first consider and do the following.

The first thing that would have to be accomplished is to totally understand each other's beliefs and religions. You need to know how devoted the other is to following the conduct and rules of their beliefs. Put aside the love and caring that you have for one another and the thought that you all are marrying outside of each other's religion. First understand the religion completely. Once you have done this and discuss it with your partner, start making some decisions. The first would be if one of you would convert to the other's religion. If this is the case, would it be something that they would continue or would they get tired of it and want to revert back. Whoever decides to change, give them time and see if it feels right for them. I am not talking about only a few months. It may take longer than a year to figure out if this is a good move. Remember, we are trying to build the foundation for a marriage and potentially a family.

If there is no conversion by anyone, then start with the rest of the decisions. First, how will each of you practice your religion? Will you all go about celebrating separately or will you both embrace each other's religion? Will you all celebrate important religious holidays together or not and how will that affect your relationship? Will you all share wonderful experiences you have had in your religious life with each other or will you not feel that you can share that with each other? The next big hurdle is how are the children going to be brought up? If you can't decide on one or the other, maybe it is best not to have children. Are you both ready to live a life without children? Even though children can decide on their own what they will practice, will it cause arguments or resentment in the household?

If these issues are one hundred percent clear and there is an understanding that can last a lifetime, then I think marriage could work. Knowing well that there will always be a separation between you both will be tough to handle though. In most circumstances, I would say that for a marriage to last, the odds would be much more in your favor if both of you had the same religious beliefs. Having the same beliefs allows the family unit to be stronger, having one clear path to follow. It allows for celebrating religious times together and allows the family to pray together, helping the children understand the importance of having good core religious belief. Having said this, I know my wonderful friends would not change one aspect of their lives as the joy and the love that they have known has shaped their lives and will never be forgotten.

CHAPTER 17

IF IT COMES DOWN TO DIVORCE

I hate to admit but it seems that there are sometimes that marriages end up in divorces anyway, no matter how good you may think it is. I recently had a friend that has six adopted children get served with divorce papers. He had to begin again. However, even in this time of difficulty, he knew who came first: The children. So if you are to get a divorce, let's go over this sequence of events and get down to how it should be done.

Notice I say 'How it should be done' and I did not say "How your lawyer would want you to have it done." Getting a divorce is a separation between the husband and the wife, not a separation between the parents and the children. The children seem to be the ones to get the biggest impact of them all. They are the ones that have to adapt to not have a mother or a father around. Their whole future is ahead of them and to not be able to have both parents there is a very big setback.

So what about the lawyer? Well, we have to remember that lawyers charge an arm and a leg per hour. If they could, and they can, they would charge you both arms and both legs and possibly a vital organ. The more time they spend on your divorce, the more they make. The more they can get the other person, usually the husband, to give, the more their cut is of the whole thing. So be sensible and work together, even in this time of bitterness. Try to settle things before going to an attorney and then use only one attorney to accomplish the deed. The idea is not to hurt anyone with the divorce, but simply to end the marriage.

During the process, you will be dividing things up and splitting them. Most of the time I guess people can sort things out ok. However, people do argue about things like televisions, sofas, computers and other material items. My advice is simple, whether or not you would like something or not, leave it where the children are to be so that they don't have to suffer any more. An adult can regroup and start over. The children have to make due with what is left behind. Of course a person has to get some things, but keep it down to personal things only. If approached from this position, there are two things that you are making perfectly clear. The first is that you are putting the children as your main priority. The second is that you are willing to make the process easier, and will in turn have a better relationship over all the years that you will have to relate with your ex-spouse.

Why does it seem so hard for people to have a peaceful divorce? What is the joy in having a rough and turbulent time in separating? In essence, you are trying to solve a problem, supposedly, but inadvertently, create another cauldron of pain. I happen to believe that many times, one of the partners begins to listen to the advice of close friends and relatives and then has second thoughts on how to deal with the separation. For instance, one of my friends seemed to have everything in line with the decisions clear cut. However, once the day came for signing the termination papers, it did not happen. Why? Simply that his ex was now wanting more. Strictly, I believe, a result of too many conversations telling her to be greedier.

Now, in opposition to this, another friend of mine has had a much better result. Both of them respecting each other and not wanting to hurt each other any further, they both came to an agreement and did the divorce the way civilized people should do it. It creates a much better relationship for the future and you avoid creating any enemies. No one knows for sure what the future holds for one, so why create problems for oneself when it is not necessary? Many people do end up getting back together.

Once it is done, keep a friendly relationship with your ex, especially if children are involved. Please do the children a favor and keep them away from being the liaisons for both of you. Stress is not one thing that children handle well all the time. They should not be placed in such situations. Make sure that everything that was agreed to still happens.

CHAPTER 18

PUTTING IT ALL TOGETHER

By this time, having read this book, you can put together the puzzle of what it may take to make a relationship work. Many of the major topics of interest that come up during a marriage have been mentioned. There is, no doubt, many other situations that can never be completely covered. Many of the intricacies that make up the human mind of ideas can never fully be realized in one book alone. This book however, if followed, and if put into practice, can benefit any marriage. It will minimize your stress and hopefully teach you how to deal better with those stressful situations when they randomly pop into your life. I can tell you that no one is ever perfect; you can only strive for that unreachable goal in a marriage. When the effort is there, and is made by both the husband and the wife, the reality is that a marriage is the best thing that can happen to a person. The chance to live with your partner, raise kids together and hopefully live to see your grandchildren run around, is more than anyone could ever ask for.

As we look back, we can see how patience is important in anything we do. Daily sacrificing ones' selfish wants to allow the family's needs to come first is something that we constantly must remind ourselves to do. If there is one thing that you can do, if nothing else, is to be honest. Honesty reigns above all. Honesty will help you make the right decisions. If I could wish anything for all of you it would be this: May all the respect in the world be showered onto you so that you may distribute it equally among everyone else. Show respect to your wife, your children, your parents, your in-laws, your neighbors and yourself.

Let's remember that during our short lifetime, we have to be able to pass on to our children the knowledge that will help make this world a better place to live. What better way of teaching our children than right at home with a mother and a father that know how to work together? Teaching them that love and respect starts at home and that a marriage is something to treasure will go a long way in their lives and in their children's lives. Let's see if together we can make this world better, one marriage at a time.

CHAPTER 19

FROM A WIFE'S PERSPECTIVE

I have read my husband's book and share his views and opinions. I would like to add a few brief notes of my own:

I am a Catholic and daily prayer gives me the strength to deal with everyday stress. As a wife and parent, I worry about the well being of my family and have found that my faith in God gives me peace of mind.

Don't allow your temper to affect your health or happiness. We all have stressful situations like a bad day at work, a sick child, a sick parent, or an unexpected expense like a leaky roof or car accident. It is vital not to get angry about the situation and look for possible solutions. No one likes to hear constant complaints or get yelled at. Getting angry does not solve the problem but can create health issues like high blood pressure and ulcers. Also, yelling at a spouse or child creates a barrier to communication. Your family will need you but cannot come to you for fear of getting yelled at. Do your best and teach your children how to handle stress by your example.

Sacrifice brings happiness. I feel that my children are my priority, then my husband, and finally myself. Making any sacrifice for them to see a smile on their face fills my heart with joy. We have all heard the saying, "It is better to give than to receive." When you give of yourself, you gain so much love and happiness that it doesn't feel like a sacrifice.

Spend family time together. Do whatever your kids enjoy. Watch TV together, have water balloon fights, play board games, make up your own games, sing together, bake desserts, make a treasure hunt where the treasure is filled with water guns or ice cream sandwiches, go swimming, walking, paint a room, or simply play video games. It doesn't matter what you do as long as there is some family time. Create family traditions with your immediate family, extended family, and friends. Children grow up quickly, so make them a priority in your life.

I wish you love and happiness . May God bless you and your families for a long and happy life together.

ABOUT THE AUTHOR

David Cruz has a wide range of interests, but for his first book, there was no question he was going to write about what is at the core of his beliefs; having the mental tools to have a strong family bond. He enjoys his work as a Family Physician, especially working closely with the patients and his peers. He is happily married with three wonderful children. He would like for this to be the beginning for a series of books.

David H. Cruz, M.D.

NOTES
CHAPTER 1
THE BEGINNING

NOTES
CHAPTER 2
PATIENCE

NOTES
CHAPTER 3
CHOOSING THE RIGHT PARTNER

NOTES
CHAPTER 4
HONESTY

NOTES
CHAPTER 5
JEALOUSY

How To Keep A Marriage Together

NOTES
CHAPTER 6
SELFISHNESS

David H. Cruz, M.D.

NOTES
CHAPTER 7
COMMUNICATION

NOTES
CHAPTER 8
IMPROVING YOURSELF

NOTES
CHAPTER 9
RAISING THE CHILDREN

NOTES
CHAPTER 10
SACRIFICE

NOTES
CHAPTER 11
ACHIEVING HAPPINESS

NOTES
CHAPTER 12
SEXUAL RELATIONSHIP

NOTES
CHAPTER 13
DON'T RUN AWAY FROM YOUR PROBLEMS

NOTES
CHAPTER 14
MONEY

NOTES
CHAPTER 15
LIFE CHANGES – CHANGE WITH IT

NOTES
CHAPTER 16
DIFFERENT RELIGIONS

NOTES
CHAPTER 17
IF IT COMES DOWN TO DIVORCE

https://diplomatie.belgium.be/

Kingdom of Belgium
Federal Public Service
**Foreign Affairs, Foreign Trade, and
Development Cooperation**

BAIT AL AMANAH
House of Trust

https://baitalamanah.com/

Center for
Market
Education

https://marketedu.me/

This research project was initiated by the Embassy of the Kingdom of Belgium to Malaysia and Brunei, in the person of H.E. Mr Pascal Gregoire, and jointly conducted by the Center for Market Education and Bait Al-Amanah.

The research was graciously supported by the Atlas Network and C.I. Holdings Berhad.

The authors would like to thank Prof Dr Fatimah binti Kari, Prof Datuk Dr Denison Jayasooria and Ms Wan Ya Shin for their valuable inputs presented during the webinar *Re-Examining Urban Poverty*, which was the initial event of the current project, held on 15 April 2021. The recording is available here: https://www.youtube.com/watch?v=CDsUP2iAt08&t=2972s.

NOTES
CHAPTER 18
PUTTING IT ALL TOGETHER

NOTES
CHAPTER 19
FROM A WIFE'S PERSPECTIVE